# Unfinished Lives

## Also by Michael Miller

*The Joyful Dark*
*The Singing Inside*
*Darkening the Grass*
*Into This World*
*Lifelines*
*The Different War*
*In the Mirror*
*Asking the Names*
*Waking in the Dark*
*Entering the Day*

# UNFINISHED LIVES

## MICHAEL MILLER

PINYON PUBLISHING
Montrose, Colorado

Copyright © 2021 by Michael Miller

All rights reserved. Except as permitted under the U.S. Copyright Act of 1976, no part of this publication may be reproduced, distributed, or transmitted in any form or by any means, or stored in a database or retrieval system, without the prior written permission of the publisher, except for brief quotations in articles, books, and reviews.

Design by Susan Entsminger

Photograph of Michael Miller by Mary Miller

First Edition: 2021

Pinyon Publishing
23847 V66 Trail, Montrose, CO 81403
www.pinyon-publishing.com

Library of Congress Control Number: 2020951581
ISBN: 978-1-936671-72-4

*For William Leo Coakley*

# Contents

## I

Shallows at Dusk   3
The Marsh   5
Dawn in Amherst   6
Clear Light   7
In the Examining Room   8
Cutting the Bread   9
Willows in April   10
Leavings   11
Dusk   12

## II

A Long Way from Ireland   17

## III

Sightings   39
Verge   40
Shadows on the Rug   41
Preparation   42
First In Line   43
Continuing   44

The Day Waiting   45
Hummingbird   46
Imagining the Flowers   47

## IV

Unfinished   51

*Seek those images
That constitute the wild,
The lion and the virgin,
The harlot and the child*

—W. B. Yeats

I

## SHALLOWS AT DUSK

Leaving the city,
Packing our memories
In suitcases without locks,
The great blue heron
Was our first blessing
When we arrived
In a quiet New England town,
Our small son
Walking between us
To the algaed pond
Where the heron descended
Over the pines to land
In the shallows at dusk,
Its wide wings
Closing like a cloak,
Drawing us into
A place beyond definition.
How naturally we surrendered
To the heron's grace,
This long-billed wader
Ignoring us in the silence
Of its routine—
High-stepping into the water
To hunt the carp.
Captivated by this ritual
We waited for the catch,
The calm water shattering,
The flame-colored carp
Wriggling in air,
Ensnared in a scissor of bill.
It was more than life,

More than death,
More than our expectations
In a new place.

# THE MARSH

As quietly as the island of ferns
Waving for me to enter
I stepped into the marsh,
My boots sinking slowly,
A measure of peace to come.
Not a sound, not a movement
From the red-wings
Perched on the cattails,
The white egret
Beneath a swamp magnolia,
The secrets of existence
In its folded wings.
Not wanting to startle it
I stopped, sensing
I was close enough,
Knowing that the distance
Between us allowed me
To love more, to love longer,
To keep this moment
In the corner of memory.

## DAWN IN AMHERST

The raccoon lay by the road,
One foreleg bent upon the other
As if attempting to outrun death.
I counted the rings on its tail,
Stared at its triangular face
With a mask of the night.
The raccoon died in the dark
In front of the Dickinson house
With tall windows facing the sunrise.
I bent down to look closer
And imagined I was Emily,
My soul reaching out.
How quickly I began
To love the raccoon!
Was it crossing the road
To return to its mate,
Its nocturnal forage ended?
The raccoon came to life inside me,
Its wide black feet ready
To resume its journey.

# CLEAR LIGHT

A welcomed dreamless sleep,
No monsters, no violence;
Six hours of needed peace
That lead into clear light
And the greeting of birdsong.
How long would perfection
Grace my day,
Fill me with the joy
Of being alive?
There are questions
I no longer ask,
Answers I no longer need.
Contentment is
A surprise of yellow
Darting from a low branch
Into a cloud of leaves.

# IN THE EXAMINING ROOM

Under the unobstructed light
In the examining room,
After a clear explanation
Of the possibilities
And a swab of iodine,
The long needle
Was inserted between the bones
Of my left knee,
The cortisone injected,
The fluid drained.
I gazed at the concentration
Of the kindly doctor,
At his shapely hands.
I thought of your hands
Touching me in candlelight,
Then closed my eyes
In the splendor of the moment.

# CUTTING THE BREAD

The rectangular loaf of sourdough
Is waiting on the cutting board
For the long knife.
I will cut it carefully,
Each fresh slice ready for
The toaster, my first step
Toward the perfection
Elusive in our lives,
In our marriage.
Now I cut the first perfect slice
For you, the second for me.
We will eat them together
At the round cherry table;
You will have butter;
I, marmalade.

# WILLOWS IN APRIL

The pale greening of willows
In April reminds me of you,
Your gradual disclosures
With their aura of shadings
That draw me again
As if we had just met
Without the ambivalence
That moves through the small
And large holes in a marriage.
We are still together,
The willows are leafing out,
The wind strokes their tassels.

# LEAVINGS

In late autumn
When the lingering birds
Continue their songs
The light grows darker
And leads me toward the garden
Emptied of blossoms
Where we stood with reverence
For all things in decline.
On the yellowing meadow
A lonely eagle feather;
We brought it
To our small house,
Placed it on the windowsill
Beside the smooth white stone
From the pond
Where we swam this summer
With our strokes
In perfect harmony
On the longest day of the year.
"Remember," the birds sing.

# DUSK

No hum from distant traffic,
No wind disturbing the leaves,
Not even the soothing call
Of a mourning dove,
Nothing except the silence
Before the Pelham Hills
With an apple orchard beside us,
The stone church behind us.
The bell chimes on the hour,
The beginning of time,
The ending of time.
Then the far away whistle,
The train approaching,
The brick station.
Not long enough our time,
Not long enough in this place
Where our spirits take their
First step toward forever.

II

# A LONG WAY FROM IRELAND

### I

When his sister followed
That rogue leprechaun,
The little man of shadow and sin
Into the changeling dark of death,
His eleven-year-old life
Changed forever in that
Unbearable year in Dublin.
Loneliness, his unwelcomed sibling,
Consumed him through
The silence of months;
Nothing could replace
Kathleen, his twin.

## II

His red-haired wife
Left a letter on his dresser
With no return address,
His son fled from
Their small college town
To San Francisco,
Estrangement in his heart.
But Patrick goes on,
Writing, teaching,
Combing his hair before sleep
For the women he might
Meet in his dreams.

## III

"Patrick McVeigh!" said his
Short-tempered wife entering
The Shamrock Pub as he looked up
From his pint knowing what
Would follow. The Shamrock
Is gone, Megan is gone,
And when he drinks past midnight
They appear at intervals,
Each warming his soul
In his house of the cold,
In his rooms of aloneness.

## IV

Adrift in the lamplight
He closed his eyes on the day
But not the past;
Patrick viewed his life
From different angles—
He sought perspective
Instead of memory addressing
What seemed to be.
Did his tracks in the snow
Disappear before the snow?
Questions abound,
Answers hidden.

## V

He touches the gold cross
Around his neck, a man at peace
With the possibilities in the night.
He dreams of a rose bush,
A hummingbird hovering over
The petals opened wide,
Its wings a blur of miracles.
"I'm a hummingbird, a rose,"
He says upon waking,
Joy bringing him into the day.

## VI

*A hummingbird, a rose,*
He wrote with his fountain pen,
His small, neat cursive
Bold on the page.
"Pay attention to your dreams,"
Professor O'Malley had told him
When Patrick asked about
Original subject matter.
And now, at his age,
He paid closer attention,
Fearful of repetition
Stealing into this poems.
He thought of the hummingbird,
The rose, and how he would
Make them his own,
Flying and opening
In unexpected places.

## VII

Poverty was never poverty
To him in the presence
Of his Mother's warmth.
By the stone fireplace
She told stories
Of milkmaids, pipers, leprechauns
While his Father
Nodded with approval.
Patrick never wanted
The stories to end,
He continued them in bed,
Speaking softly in the dark.

## VIII

To wake from a dream
Of his sister, of Kathleen
In full-bodied womanhood
Digging in a garden
Filled him with bittersweet joy,
Led him into the dawn with
Illusions rubbed from his eyes.
"Kathleen," he whispers
And rises from bed,
Leaving his dream
In the wrinkled sheets.

## IX

His dark blue flannel shirt
Fits snugly. Too many pints
Patrick thinks, looking at
His reflection in the mirror:
Thick curly hair streaked with gray,
Circles beneath his blue eyes.
He turns away, picks up
His briefcase and hurries to class,
His eager students waiting.
"Be kind, be encouraging,"
He says, and love rises
Inside him, love for
His long ago innocence,
His hunger to learn.

## X

In the changing hour
When the fireflies blink messages
He can never decipher
And the great horned owl
Calls from the neighboring wood,
Patrick sits on the tilting porch
And thinks of Ireland,
Of Sullivan joining the IRA
For the cause worth dying for.
He refused to join.
Ireland was not for him.

## XI

Patrick wants a woman
His own age with the richness
Of years, an independent woman
Who brings a history
To his bed, someone to replace
Megan if that is possible.
He would like to dream about
A woman other than his wife,
His ex-wife. But Megan has
Lasted, his love has lasted,
No matter if she is living
In Dublin, her old life a new life
That rouses his curiosity.

## XII

In the emptiness of his house,
In the silence of foreboding
And the stillness
Like an opened grave,
Patrick lies on the couch
Where Megan came to him
To make love. Now all things
Lead back to Megan: his neighbor
In the stone house in Dublin,
His adventurous friend at
Thirteen, his wife at eighteen.
Now she is amputated from his life.

## XIII

At his Mother's funeral
Patrick leaned over
The open coffin and touched
Her cheek which felt like wax;
A powerful impulse passed
Through him: to climb in,
To lie down beside her
And put his arm
Around her waist.
Mothers, sons, an invisible
Umbilical cord between them
That Patrick never wanted
To cut, his Mother returning
In dreams, in thoughts
Of his own death
In a country she would
Never visit despite
His gentle urging.

## XIV

Into the blue river of his vein
The needle was inserted,
The blood drawn:
Life taken, life tested,
The results in three days.
But how would they check
The condition of his soul
Without Megan? Always friendly
But keeping his distance,
Wary of intimacy,
Patrick wished he could
Open like the blossoms
In his garden, no longer
Needing his disguises
Of laughter and language,
The jovial Irishman
Raising his glass.

## XV

Leaning back in his rocker
On the porch after another
Bourbon chased by beer,
Patrick asks the questions.
Does he want love
Or the dream of love?
Which answer will his
Heart tilt him toward?
Closing his eyes, almost
Drunk enough to embrace
Reality, Patrick prizes
Uncertainty, believing truth
The assassin waiting for him.

## XVI

They are buried side by side,
His Mother, Father, and Kathleen,
The lichen growing on their gravestones.
Tonight he yearns for his Mother,
The wisdom in her words—
"You can manage, Paddy"—
When he asked for help
In those childhood years.
He has managed,
Managed to make the wrong choices,
The right choices, and find
The uneven road between,
His Mother's words
Embedded in him.

## XVII

Complicated love he says
When he thinks of Megan—
The complications are in him,
The boy trembling
In the confession booth
Now the man still trying
To break free.
Patrick whispers ten Hail Marys
Each time he passes a church,
Closer to guilt than God.

## XVIII

That singular night appeared
In his thoughts as he tried to sleep.
Sex was all they wanted
When they left the bar;
Patrick felt utterly free,
The violator of vows,
The joyful sinner.
Only once did he think
Of Megan pacing the room
After her lacerating words.
Sex healed Patrick's wounds,
His crucifix silent in his pocket.

## XIX

Patrick reached for his pen
And began a letter to God.
He told him of the white field
Without a footprint, of the purity
Absent from his life,
Of the birch bark unfolding
Like a scroll with invisible
Answers to his questions.
Patrick left the letter unfinished—
With no address for God.

III

# SIGHTINGS

The friendship in his dreams
Sustains him through his days,
Through his old age
He never expected to reach,
A quiet man who built his life
With books and birds,
Who wanted a bookcase
For his seventh birthday,
A birdfeeder for his eighth.
Solitary by nature,
An avid birdwatcher since boyhood,
He lists his sightings
In a blue notebook each day,
Thrushes rising
Between his sentences.
He would like to die
While looking at the scarlet tanager
On the low birch branch
Or while walking with
The silver-haired woman
Appearing in his dreams,
Her kindness drawing out his own.
He tells her about the goldfinch
He saw yesterday, an offspring
Of his angels, and the
Black-masked cedar waxwing
Darting from hedge to hemlock.

# VERGE

Turning on the bedside lamp,
A singular sun she can
Count upon, she blinks her way
Into the day, covers one eye,
Then the other, delighted that
Her sight has stopped deteriorating,
An elderly woman
On the verge of blindness.

She will practice braille,
Touching the raised marks
With a new tenderness.
She will use her cane,
walking carefully toward
The birdsong in the trees.
She will find the grosbeak first,
Its song becoming her song.

# SHADOWS ON THE RUG

By the window with flowers of frost
He leans back in his worn chair
Too tired to read any longer;
His eyes close, his eyes open,
The shadows on the rug
Are islands that will disappear
When he turns off the lamp—
Darkness that familiar place.

For two years he has not
Made love with his wife,
Desire buried in the cemetery
Without a gravestone.
Wanting to live for her
He is not ready to die,
Knowing the bottom of love
Can never be reached.

# PREPARATION

Preparing for death,
Their own, each other's,
They sometimes speak of it,
Sometimes are more content
In that windowless room
Of silence.
They try to live fully,
To find the light
Beyond the dark,
The beauty in the moment.
He gazes at her hands
Before waking her—
Another day!
And joy opens,
The blossom within.

# FIRST IN LINE

Without the need for words
She extended the plate
With turkey and mashed potatoes,
A middle-aged woman
With kindness in her eyes.
If only he could say thank you,
If only she was real!
He has never had enough
Food or kindness,
An old man with
A child's hunger churning within.
But in the cafeteria of dreams,
Under the ample light,
He is always first in line,
Gripping his tray,
Ready to be served,
Eager to eat.

# CONTINUING

In old age harmony hides
In his gray beard,
Opposition is rampant
In her wayward hair.
But they continue,
Depending on each other
For small things, large things.
As they approach death
Loyalty has become love.

# THE DAY WAITING

His full-throated reply
To the hermit thrush
On the sugar maple fills him
With his portion of wonder,
Dispelling the loneliness
In his eighty-seventh spring.
Vision and mobility
Have diminished,
Death travels in his thoughts
But desire drives him on:
There is more to reach out to.
His agenda is everything,
Everything beyond the self
In the day waiting,
Each slow step
Taking in a world.

# HUMMINGBIRD

The hummingbird, ruby-throated,
Against the stark white sky
Is poised for flight
On the upright card
On the kitchen table.
She cannot find the words
For its iridescence
Or needle-like bill;
She cannot find the words
For her accumulating losses
Kept in a hatbox in the closet.
But she can imagine
Flying like a hummingbird,
Celebrating her birthday with
A card she bought for herself.

# IMAGINING THE FLOWERS

With seven pens of different colors
He draws flowers in a large sketchbook,
Beginning each imaginary flower
Before sleep and hoping
To continue after waking,
To finish in a week or a month,
Finding delight in old age
As his hand breathes life
Into stems, petals, blossoms,
Dignifying the work
Through peace and silence.
He draws with the freedom
In routine, discovering ideas
In shapes and colors,
Making every flower unique,
Never giving them a name.

IV

# UNFINISHED

### I

In the winter of despair,
Uncertain of where to turn,
He avoids the presence
Of others, preferring
The birches for company,
The bare branches confirming
His need to strip away
His postures, his disguises,
Then dig into the earth
Of self to find
The essential roots
That will allow him
To approach the clay.

## II

Ignoring his recurring fear
Of death and the madness
Crowding his blood
He turns quietly to her,
Her richness the fullness
Of summer he will sculpt
Through the night,
His passion rising into vision.

III

No one can interfere with
His art, his only obstacle
Is himself, his arrogance,
His doubt, the opposing
Forces that clash inside him.
He needs to avoid
Repetition, to discover
A shape beyond thought,
Beyond life as he knows it.

## IV

Once he knelt and prayed
To the clay, asking for a sign
Of the shape within it.
He could live without words
But not without the simplicity
Beyond the self,
The imaginative leap,
The peace after the passion.

## V

On some occasions he speaks
to the clay, whispering
"Breathe!" as if he were
Holding a newborn;
His left hand strength,
His right hand gentleness,
Both hands leading the way.

## VI

At two in the morning
He listens to Beethoven,
Shaping the clay as the music
Lifts him into a realm
Beyond understanding,
A realm of focused energy.
He sculpts with
A sustained rapidity:
Substance becomes form,
Contours emerge
And satisfaction,
A dormant companion,
Stirs within him.

## VII

The mirror reflects
His haphazard white hair,
Unruly eyebrows,
Lip tilted down
Toward the unwanted grave,
But there is still
The unexpected composure,
The elusive curves of originality
As he translates his rough edges
Into his work.
He would like to live
Inside his sculpture,
To see his image
Standing before it,
To reach out from the shape
And invite himself to enter.

## VIII

Smoothing over his fingerprints
In the clay, wanting
No trace of his hand,
Perspective grows
As he continues,
Each angle revealing a newness,
Each work leading him
Toward something sustaining,
A quiet sense of renewal.

## IX

Last night he dreamt of
The marble quarries in Carrara,
Of Donatello, Michelangelo,
Canova, of another time,
Another place.
He tries to begin each day
With freshness.
Once in his studio
The discontent stirs
Within him, rising as he
Stares at a sculpture—
He is never satisfied.

## X

Never has he forgotten
His ninth summer when he stood
Before the marble lovers,
Their smooth bodies embracing
Beneath the bright light.
After the guard passed through
The gallery he reached out
And stroked the marble slowly.
Suddenly he felt lifted
Out of himself.

## XI

On the wooden table
Beside the tall windows
His new sculpture stands,
Three weeks in the making.
He resists the impulse
To smash it against
The concrete floor,
To see the elongated body
Break into pieces,
Mismatched pieces that
Are a part of his life.

## XII

He tried to mold his marriage
As if it were clay,
To shape it into an extension
Of their feelings, their thoughts,
Drawing them together,
Keeping them close
When they needed to be apart.
Love was measured by acts:
Kindness, tenderness, loyalty.

## XIII

Death is before him,
Behind him, but not inside him
When he is working the clay
Into a shape he imagines,
A form with the life surging
Through him into his hands,
Large, wide hands leading him
As he creates,
His feelings wedded to thought.

## XIV

Now her older body possessed
A new beauty he wanted to sculpt,
The ridges and valleys
Distinct in his mind.
She would pose if he asked,
Stand ten feet away
Or lie on the couch facing him.
But he wanted to work
From memory, to let his mind
Create a loveliness that would last.

## XV

The giving, the taking away,
The mound of clay
Never meant to remain the same;
Handfuls and scraps covered
The table, a torso gradually
Emerged, the shape instilled
With ideas from his hands.
When he thought it was done
He stepped back,
Looking instead of creating,
The sculpture waiting
To be named.

## XVI

In his cluttered studio
Without a clock
He works through the night,
All his sculptures become one—
There is no result
But a continual beginning.
What he has learned
He tries to forget,
Loving the malleable clay,
Shaping it to his desire,
Not able to stop,
Telling himself the work
Will never be finished.

www.ingramcontent.com/pod-product-compliance
Lightning Source LLC
Chambersburg PA
CBHW021023090426
42738CB00007B/887